Portable & Home hosted Learning Management Systems

DHUNY RIYAD

DEDICATION

To the community of educators who are yet to discover how a Learning Management System (LMS) can reduce their workload and improve their efficiency.

To all educators and students located in remote areas where internet connectivity is a luxury.

CONTENTS

ACKNOWLEDGMENTS

As strange as this would appear, I have to acknowledge people that I do not know personally.
I have to thank the Open Source community without which none of this would have been possible.
Special thanks to Nicolas Martignoni for his Moodlebox project. Moodlebox is more than a
Moodle on a Raspberry Pi. It does cost the maintainer time to perform these regular updates.
I need to also acknowledge all those working in the same direction to make educational tools like
LMS more accessible to remote areas.

1 INTRODUCTION

Mobile phones and tablets are now an integral part of majority of the students' lives. In developing countries of Africa, projects like One Laptop Per Child (OLPC) (Kraemer, Dedrick, & Sharma, 2011) made computing devices more accessible to a wider audience for mobile learning. This opened new doors for online teaching and learning but the real driver was the covid-19 pandemic which forced many schools and educational institutions to adopt online leaning or blended learning.

As with any Computerization Movements (CM), this process for the education sector should be accompanied with appropriate strategies. For example, in Mauritius, primary school students have their own tablets with the school books preloaded as e-textbooks together with appropriate multimedia materials, quizzes, multiple-choice questions (MCQ) and much more to interact with. Unfortunately, the work progress, scored marks for questions and other activities are not computed or are not visible for the educator to be able to track a student's individual progress.

This is where a Learning Management System (LMS) comes in action. An LMS allow educators to set up a common repository that all students can connect to. Among the advantages, the educator can keep track of students' progress, identify those who lag behind and most importantly, all quizzes and multiple-choice questions can be automatically graded. This provides the educator with more free time to perform classroom management and track students with learning difficulties.

The Modular Object-Oriented Dynamic Learning Environment (Moodle) is one of the most popular open source LMSs available. From the official statistics of Moodle website represented below as Figure 1, Moodle had more than 182,000 active deployments in 243 countries as at March 2021.

Statistics

Sites	Courses	Users	Enrolments
182,000	35,000,000	262,000,000	1,482,000,000

Forum posts	Resources	Quiz questions	Countries
591,000,000	287,000,000	4,102,000,000	243

Figure 1: Official Moodle usage statistics.

Given Moodle's popularity, same shall be used as the only LMS throughout this book. It is of course possible to convert other LMSs into portable ones but it is beyond the scope of this book.

Many educators have learned about the advantages of LMS or experienced the benefits themselves in the past but, setting up one for use can be a daunting task as it involves some technical skills or knowhow. For example, Moodle requires a web, application and database server to operate. To get a server or to publish a content online, one would turn to a web hosting provider. Then, the difficulties that arise are of various types like: (1) free Moodle hosting providers offer services with some limitations, (2) paid hosting service providers do not offer tailor-made support for Moodle or educators, (3) the hosting cost is too high for educators without the support of their institutions, (4) educational institutions or classes do not have necessary network infrastructure to work online and (5) reluctance of educators to give it a try.

The aim of this book is to remove all the technical barriers in order to empower educators to make use of LMSs for their day to day class management. The knowledge present therein is useful to support education for remote areas, private tutors with small cohort sizes and online learning. For the majority part of the book, LMS will be run from a portable mobile computing device known as Raspberry Pi (RPI) (raspberrypi.org, 2021). RPIs are mobile computing devices that cost around US$ 39 – 85 (pimoroni, 2021). Figure 2 shows the small form factor of the Raspberry Pi which is approximately the size of a credit card.

Figure 2: Small form factor of a Raspberry Pi. The width is less than 10 cm.

The latest version of RPI is the version 4 which has a Quad core 64-bit CPU of type ARM, 2.4 and 5.0 Ghz Wi-Fi, Bluetooth 5.0, Gigabit LAN, 2 USB 3.0 ports, 2 USB 2.0 ports and 2, 4 or 8 GB of RAM.

Upcoming chapters of this book will use RPI4 and Moodle to produce either a portable LMS or a Home hosted LMS for use in the education sector. The LMS shall support up to 30 students out of the box for a medium size course. The Wi-Fi of the Raspberry Pi will be converted into an access point to allow students to connect to the device wirelessly eliminating the need for other network infrastructure.

To implement, test and build the portable LMS as per chapters in this book, readers will need the following:

1. A Raspberry Pi 4.
2. A good quality 2.5A USB-C 5v power adapter.
3. A micro SD card of at least 8 GB.
4. An RPI4 fan and heatsinks.
5. An RPI4 casing optionally with battery.
6. As optional material, a Solid-State Disk (SSD) and its USB casing / connectors.

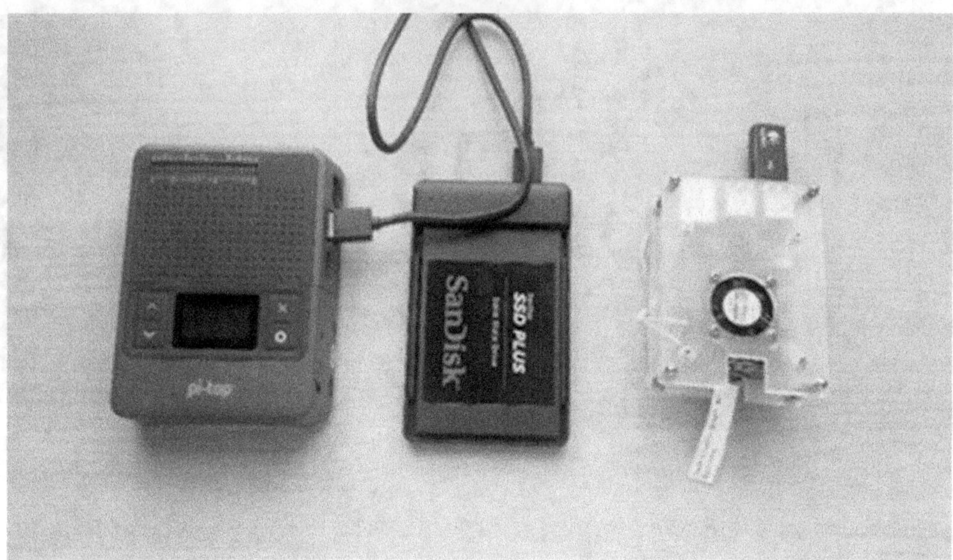

Figure 3: from left to right, RPI4 casing with battery, Solid state disk with its casing and a RPI4 casing with fan.

Figure 3 shows two different RPI4 casings, the one on the left has a battery included and can run approximately 5 hours without mains power. The casing on the right represents a standard casing with an RPI fan. RPI4 are known to have CPU throttling issues when the temperature rises, it is a good idea to have a heat sink and / or a fan.

Note: All links for referenced resources are available in the References section of this book.

2 MOODLEBOX

If you have already received your equipment listed on page 3, the easiest way to get started is to install Moodlebox on your RPI4.

Moodlebox is a project by Nicolas Martignoni and team (Moodlebox, 2021) which is a Raspberry Pi OS image with appropriate software installed to run Moodle out of the box. The installation process to get Moodlebox running is straightforward. Simply visit the Moodlebox website and download the Moodlebox Disk Image located under the *Get Moodlebox Menu*.

Once the Disk image is downloaded, you will need to burn same onto your micro SD Card before booting on your Raspberry Pi. There are a variety of tools that may be used to burn the downloaded images, namely:
1. Balena Etcher (balena, 2021).
2. Raspberry Pi Imager (Raspberry Pi, 2021).
3. Win32 Disk Imager (Sourceforge.net, 2018).

Balena Etcher

With Balena Etcher installed, simply browse the Disk Image, the micro SD Card location and click on Flash! as shown in Figure 4.

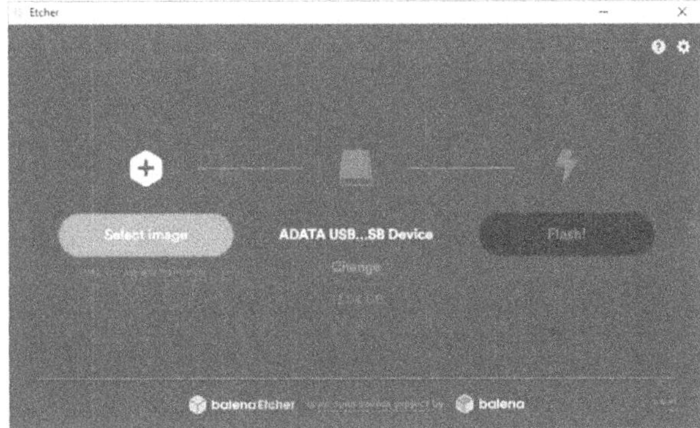

Figure 4: Balena Etcher tool to flash disk image to SD card.

Win32 Disk Imager

The Win32 Disk Imager can be used to Write a Disk Image onto a micro SD Card. This tool has the added advantage of having a Read button that can be used to backup an existing SD card image if required.

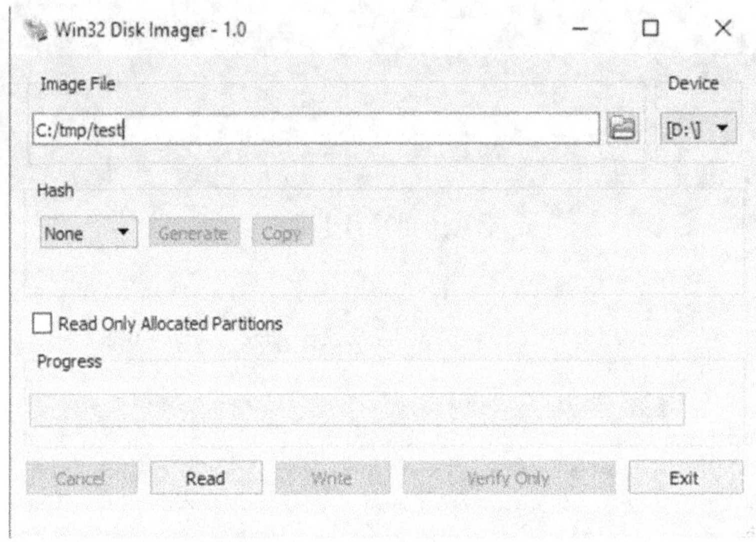

Figure 5: win32 Disk Imager has a read button to backup SD card contents.

Booting up Moodlebox

Once the image is transferred to the card, the next step is to boot the Moodlebox. To do so, insert the MicroSD card into the RPI slot and connect an Ethernet cable if you have one. Power the device and notice that the green light is blinking to indicate activity.

Connecting to Moodlebox

To connect to your Moodlebox, simply scan your Wi-Fi network with another device, a new access point should be available under the name of **Moodlebox** as shown in Figure 6. To connect to same, simply use the password **moodlebox** and you are done.

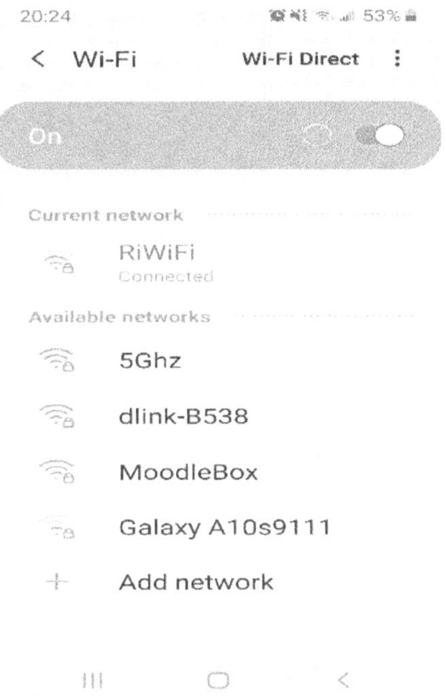

Figure 6: Moodlebox network access point.

Visiting the portable Moodle

It is possible to visit the Moodle website by using any device connected to the 'moodlebox' Wi-Fi. The next step is to open browser and type http://moodlebox.home.

3 MOODLE PLUGINS

In the previous chapter, Moodlebox was installed as an easy way to have access to a portable LMS. The LMS is empty and does not contain any course content. In this lesson, the Moodle functionalities will be extended through the use of the following plugins below:
1. Moodle Benchmark (Martignoni & Pannequin, 2020).
2. Interactive Content – H5P (Petterson, Marstrander, Jørgensen, With, & Svein-Tore, 2021).
3. Treasure Hunt (de Castro, et al., 2021), (de Castro J. , 2021).

Logging in as Administrator

To login as Administrator from the home page of Moodle, click on the Log in link present on the top right-hand corner. For Moodlebox, the username is **moodlebox** and the password is **Moodlebox4$**. Once a user is properly logged in as Administrator, the Site administration menu should be visible as shown in Figure 7.

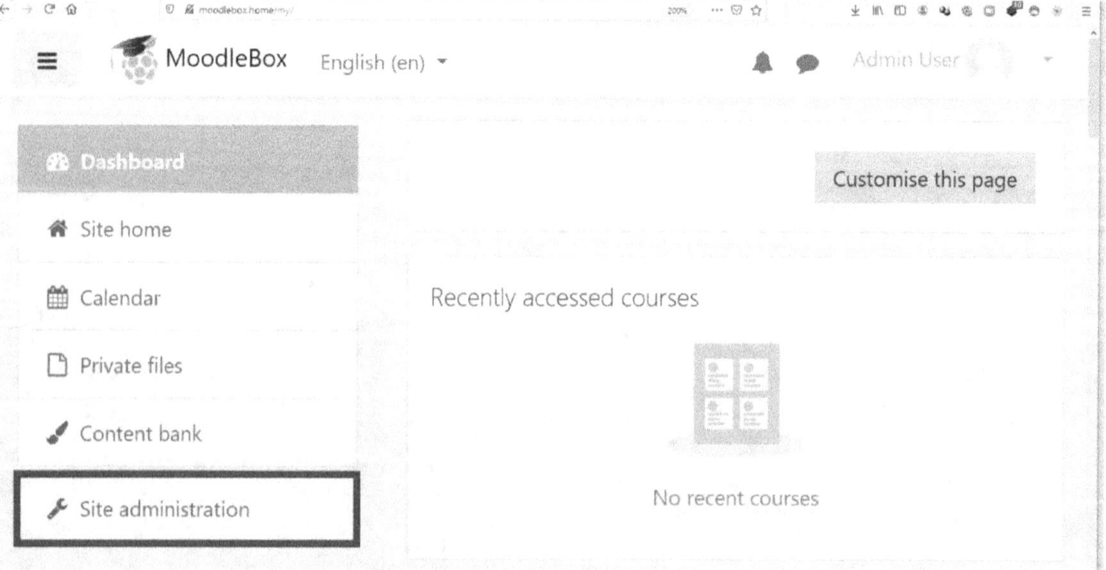

Figure 7: Administrators should have access to Site administration menu.

Create Course and add course contents

Creating courses and adding course contents are properly documented and will be skipped in this book. Readers are encouraged to create a course by clicking on the **create course** button present on the Site home page and add some course contents.

Create test content

Another way to populate a course is to create test courses. This can be done through the use of the Make test course page. To do so, Click on **Site administration** followed by the Development tab first. The highlighted links in Figure 8 will be used to create a test content.

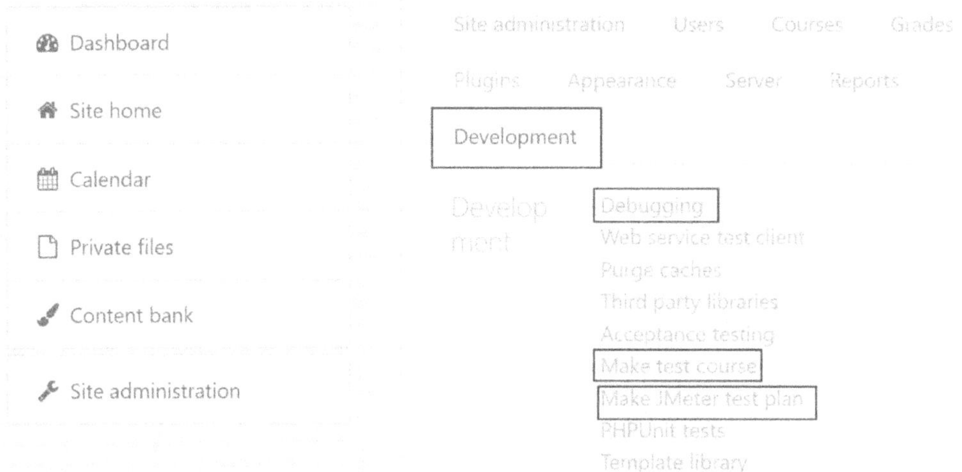

Figure 8: Development tab with Debugging and Make test course.

- To create a test course, the debugging mode should be placed on Developer mode.
- To do so, click on **Debugging**, Change **Debug Message** to **DEVELOPER.**
- Click on **Save Changes.**
- Click on **Site administration** again →**Development** tab → **Make test course.**
- From the course list set the Course Short Name to **S.**
- Set Course Full name to **Short Course** and add a course summary.
- Click on **Create Course** once done.

Moodle will take a few seconds to create the short course, click on **continue** to get access to the course contents. Notice that the Menu on the left now has Participants, Badges, Competencies Grades and Topics. The Site administration is at the bottom of the menu.

If you click on participants, you will find that 100 participants were added into the system.

To add a specific user password, Moodle requires the specification of same in its config file when generating test courses and test plans. Same will be covered in upcoming chapters.

To add contents to the newly short course created, click on a Topic (Topic 1) from the left Menu and in the top right-hand corner, you will find **Turn Editing On.** Once clicked, an edit pencil icon will appear next to the topic items. At the end of a topic, in the right-hand corner, there is a **+ add an activity or resource. Click on the +** icon to get access to resources that can be added.

A list of activities and resources as available in the current Moodle system is displayed as shown in Figure 9. Notice that there is an H5P content as the last item on the second row and there is no Treasure Hunt activity. In upcoming section, three plugins will be added, two of which will be visible in the add activity or resource list.

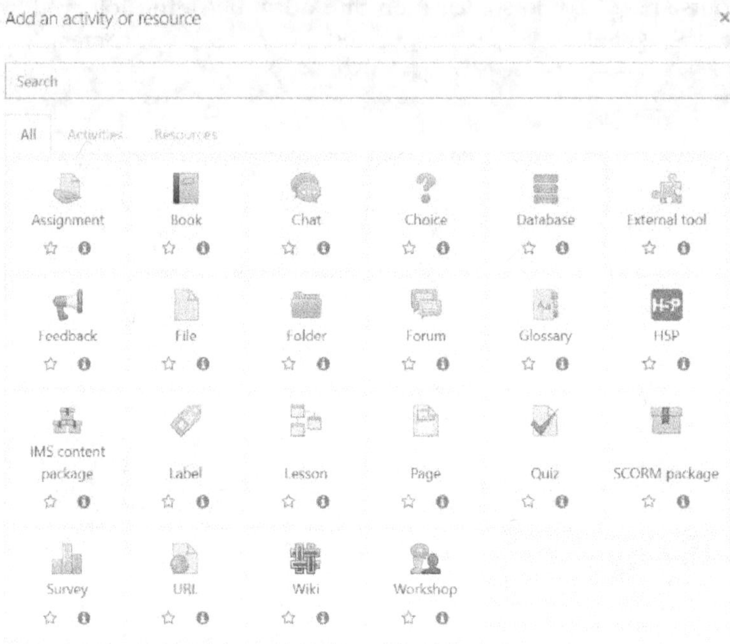

Figure 9: List of activities and resources available in Moodle.

Installing a plugin

- From the main menu available on the left, scroll down and click on the Site administration.
- Click on **Plugins tab** followed by **install plugins.**
- **Open a new tab** in your computer **browser** and visit the page https://moodle.org/plugins/.
- Search and download Moodle Benchmark from theMoodle plugins webpage.
- Return back to the Moodle plugin installer page on your moodlebox.home website, drop the zipped folder **report_benchmark** into the zipped package section and click on **install plugin from the ZIP file.**
- Click on **Continue.**
- Read the **Other Checks** section properly. An example is available in Figure 10.
- Click on **Continue** followed by **Upgrade Moodle database now** and **Continue.**

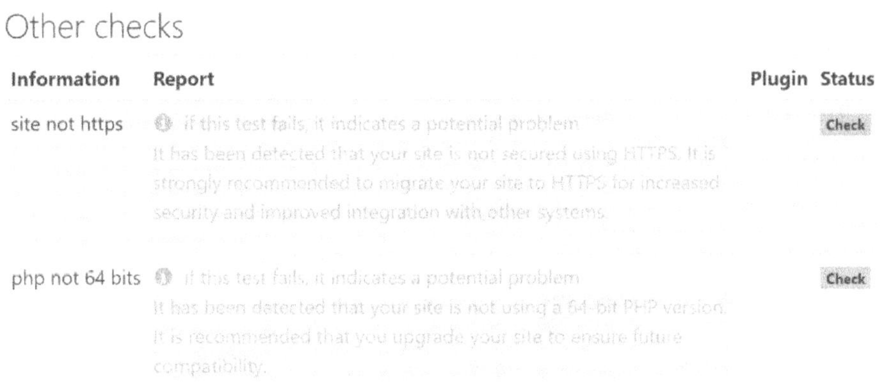

Other checks

Information	Report	Plugin	Status
site not https	⊕ if this test fails, it indicates a potential problem It has been detected that your site is not secured using HTTPS. It is strongly recommended to migrate your site to HTTPS for increased security and improved integration with other systems.		Check
php not 64 bits	⊕ if this test fails, it indicates a potential problem It has been detected that your site is not using a 64-bit PHP version. It is recommended that you upgrade your site to ensure future compatibility.		Check

Figure 10: Moodle other checks found site not https and php not 64 bits.

Moodle Benchmark

Moodle Benchmark is a reporting plugin that was added into the reporting of the Site administration panel. Click on **Site administration, Reports tab** and **Benchmark** to get access to same.

Installing Interactive Content – H5P and Treasure Hunt

- Visit the Moodle plugins webpage, search and download the Interactive Content – H5P and Treasure Hunt.
- Open the install plugins pages on Moodle and install the two plugins.
- Accept the default settings by clicking on **Save Changes** for both plugins.

Interactive Content -H5P in action

Once the two plugins are installed new activities are available under each topic. One innovative way to engage students in eLearning is through the use of interactive videos in the like of H5P. This allows educators to add questions and quizzes on top of video contents. When videos are viewed, H5P automatically pause videos at specific keyframes set in order to engage students with interactive contents. Furthermore, it allows the integration of YouTube videos directly into Moodle as embedded ones.

- Click on Site home from the menu, then click Short Course followed by Topic 1. Alternatively, open any topic. Click on **Turn Editing On** followed by **+ add an activity or resource.**
- From the list 2 new icons should appear when compared with Figure 9, namely Interactive Content and Treasure Hunt.
- Select **Interactive Content**, then in the Editor Section click on **Get** button for interactive Video. Click on **Install** to install same.
- Once installed, click on **use.**

- Under the **Add a video** section click on the **+** icon and add a YouTube Video Link.
- Next click on the **add Interactions**, a page similar to Figure 11 will be visible, try the different interactive tools available in the top row.

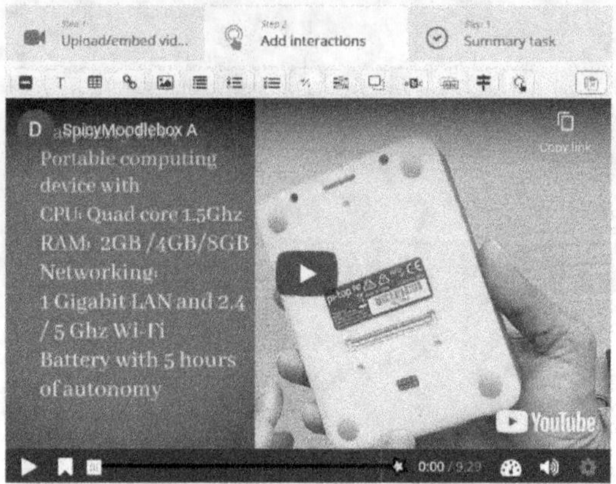

Figure 11: Add interactions tab inside Interactive contents - H5P.

4 TESTING THE PORTABLE MOODLE PERFORMANCE

There are different ways to test the performance of a Moodle. In this chapter, the Moodle Benchmark will be used to test the overall performance of the Moodle, James Chambers script will be used to test the performance of the SD Card, finally the Apache JMeter will be used to run a test plan and test the performance of a Moodle.

Moodle Benchmark
Simply run the Moodle Benchmark script present in the Site administration under the reports menu to get a detailed report on the Moodle's performance.
- **Click on Site administration → Reports → Benchmark → Start the Benchmark.**

#	Description	Time (seconds)	Acceptable limit	Critical limit
1	Moodle loading time	0.032	0.5	0.8
2	Processor processing speed	0.961	0.5	0.8
3	Reading file performance - Moodle temporary folder	0.054	0.5	0.8
4	Writing file performance - Moodle temporary folder	0.246	1	1.25
5	Reading course performance - reading speed of the database	0.097	0.75	1
6	Writing course performance - writing speed of the database	0.106	1	1.25
7	Database performance (#1)	0.016	0.5	0.7
8	Database performance (#2)	0.039	0.3	0.5
9	Login time performance for the guest account	0.099	0.3	0.8
10	Login time performance for a fake user account	0.109	0.3	0.8

Total time 1.759s

Score 176 points

Table 1: Moodle Benchmark for Moodlebox version 3.10.0 update 2021-03-20.

Table 1 shows an example results provided by Moodle Benchmark tool. The Description was truncated to maintain only the important description identifiers and information. It can be seen from the Table that item number 2, the '*Processor processing speed*' was higher than the critical limit. The overall score was 1.76 points given that the test took 1.759 seconds to run. With this test, lower scores mean better response / results from the server.

James Chambers script

The James Chambers script is executed on the portable Moodle by running a Linux shell script. To connect to the Moodlebox terminal, Secured Shell (SSH) is required. One easy way to get access to SSH is to install putty (Tatham, Lanes, Harris, & Nevins, 2020).

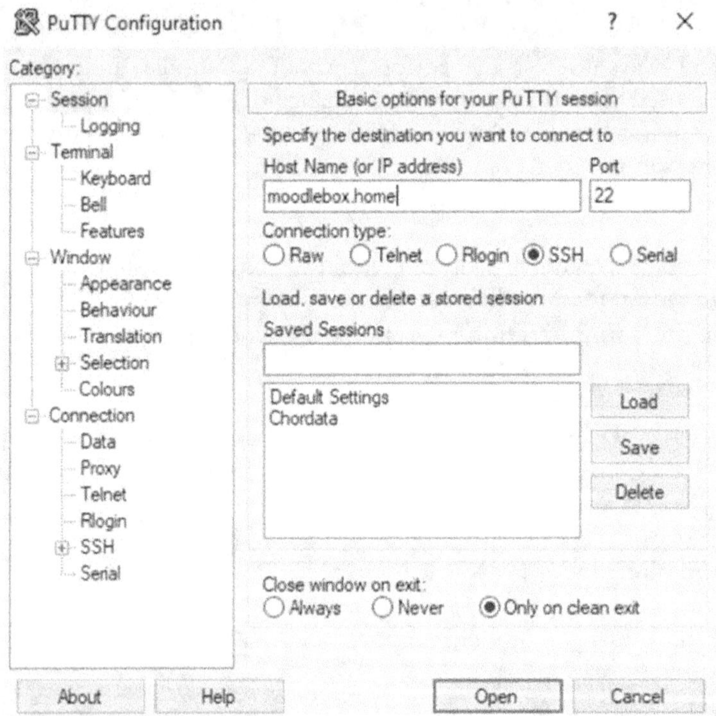

Figure 12: Putty configuration with host name as moodlebox.home.

- Open putty, in the Host Name section add Moodlebox.home as shown in Figure 12. Click on **Open.** A terminal window shall appear requesting a username and a password.
- Use **moodlebox** and **Moodlebox4$** for username and password.
- Successful login will provide access to Moodlebox shell.
- It is a good idea to do **sudo apt update && sudo apt upgrade -y** on the first run to update the Linux libraries and applications to the latest ones.
- Visit https://storage.jameschambers.com and copy the benchmark script to test the Raspberry Pi storage speed.

- The shell command is as follows:

sudo curl https://raw.githubusercontent.com/TheRemote/PiBenchmarks/master/Storage.sh | sudo bash

- This test will take a few minutes to download updates and install packages to test the disks speed of the Moodle System. The script performs some standard disk speed checks namely HDParm, dd, fio and iozone to calculate a score for the disk.

Observe the value of the Number 5 from Table 1 which represents the '*Writing course performance*'. One way to optimize the server is to find ways to improve the individual sections without degrading the performance of other items in Table 1. In upcoming chapter, the SD card will be upgraded to a fast SSD, then row 6 in Table 1 shall improve by having a lower value.

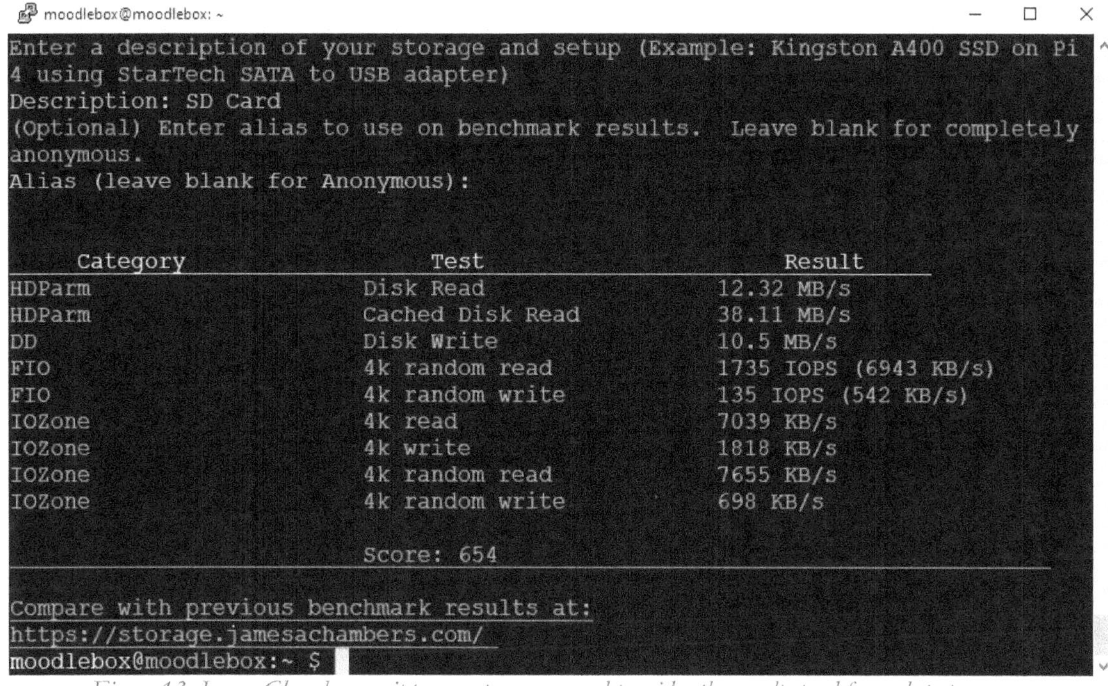

Figure 13: James Chambers script generate a score and provides the result speed for each test.

Figure 13 shows an output for an SD Card with the James Chambers score. Higher scores are better. The score can be used to compare different disk makes against their scores on the site storage.jameschambers.com.

It is possible to test a Moodle website by simulating a number of users joining a course at the same time. Apache JMeter is a stress test and performance test tool. In upcoming section, Apache JMeter will be covered.

Apache JMeter Test plan

Moodle generates test plans that can be executed with Apache JMeter. The '*make JMeter test plan*' is located in the Site administration under the development tab as shown in Figure 8.

To create a small test plan:

- Click on **Site administration** → **Development tab** → **Make JMeter test plan.**
- Read the contents present on the page carefully.
- The second paragraph states that the password for course users should be set in the config.php e.g.

$CFG->tool_generator_users_password = 'moodle';

- Copy this line and get back to SSH terminal or putty shell.
- Type **sudo nano /var/www/moodle/config.php.**
- Use the arrow keys to move to the cursor to the end of the document then paste the link (a right click may be sufficient to paste the link).
- To save the file, click on CTRL + o (the alphabet), followed by CTRL +x.
- Get back to the JMeter test plan page and select **S** as the **size of course.**
- Set the Test target course as **S.**
- Check the **update course users password.**
- Click on **Create test plan.**
- Download the **test plan** and the **users file.**

Among the two files, you have a .csv file containing email addresses and passwords. The second one is a .jmx file which contains an Apache JMeter test plan.

To run the test, you will need to install JMeter first on your computer. The installation process is beyond the scope of the book and there are some good video tutorials available on YouTube for this section (Raghav Pal, 2016). Do search on YouTube for '*JMeter Beginner Tutorial 1 – How to install Jmeter*'.

Installing and opening JMeter on Windows
- Install Java on your computer first.
- Download the latest version of Apache JMeter binaries from its website (Apache JMeter, 2021).
- **Extract** the zipped folder on your computer. In this example, we will use C:\tmp as the location folder.
- **Copy** the **.jmx** and **.csv** files from the previously downloaded section to C:\tmp.
- **Rename** the files to **ss.jmx** and **ss.csv.**
- **Rename** the extracted folder to **apache-jmeter** by removing the version numbers in the filename.
- Open the bin folder located here as C:\tmp\apache-jmeter\bin.
- Double click on jmeter, the windows batch file from the list to open Apache JMeter.
- Click on File → Open → C:\tmp\ss.jmx.
- You should have an interface similar to Figure 14.
- **Click** on **Samples per minute** and **change** the **120.0** value in the **throughput** to **180.0.**
- **Click** on the play start icon button (green arrow) to start a test.
- Notice the exclamation mark icon on the top right-hand corner and the increasing

counter when the tests are executed.
- This current method is used to check the test plan before executing same.
- Shell commands are used to execute a test plan.

Executing a test plan

The xx.jmx should be executed via the command line. On Mac and Linux, this is done by browsing the bin folder. On Windows, one easy way is to open the bin folder with File Explorer, in our case, C:\tmp\apache-jmeter\bin\, then on the address bar type **cmd**. This shall open the command prompt inside the folder. From the command prompt, type the following command to execute the test.

```
jmeter -n -j "C:\tmp\logfiless.log" -t "C:\tmp\ss.jmx" -Jusersfile="C:\tmp\ss.csv" -l "C:\tmp\result-ss.csv" -e -o "C:\tmp\ss"
```

Code snippet 1: Command on prompt to execute JMeter test.

The command in Code snippet 1 will save a log file as logfiles.log, will use ss.jmx as the test plan, will use credentials in Juserfile, save the results in result-ss.csv and produce an HTML report in the folder c:\tmp\ss.

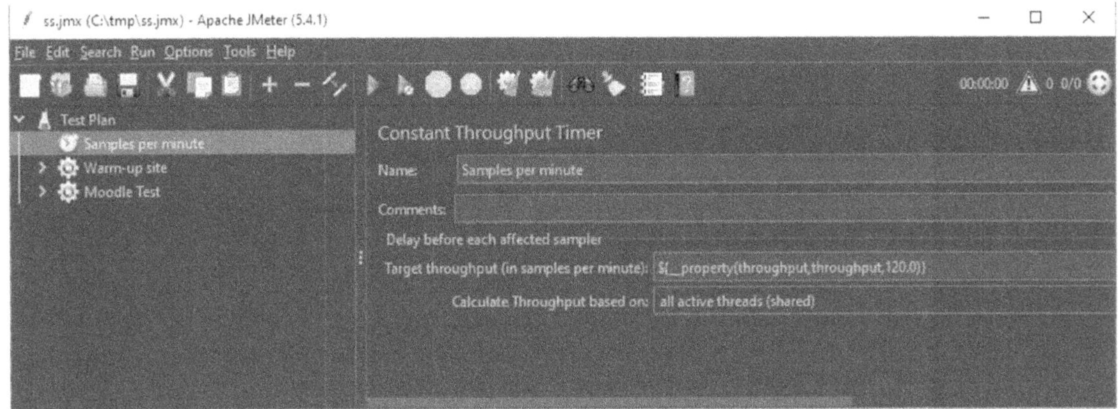

Figure 14: Apache JMeter with the generated test plan.

If the test plan is executed successfully, you should have a detailed HTML report similar to the one in Figure 15. An Apdex value close to 1 indicates an excellent user satisfaction and one below 0.5 indicates an unacceptable user satisfaction.

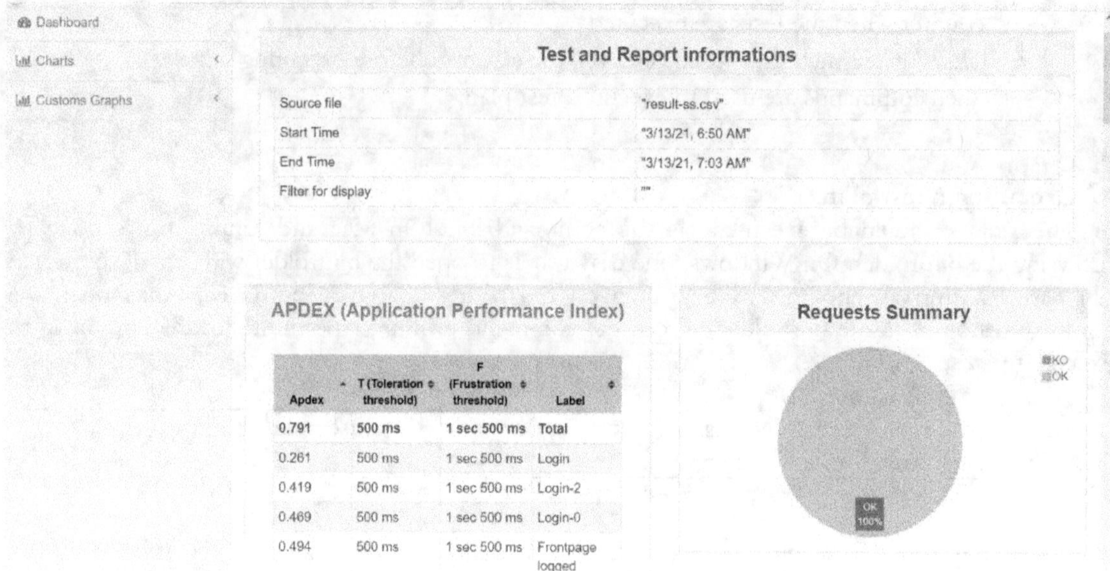

Figure 15: Apache JMeter report.

The Apache JMeter dashboard includes some interesting charts worth reviewing. For example, Figure 16 shows the number of hits per second during the whole test. The Maximum hits per second were approximately 6.5.

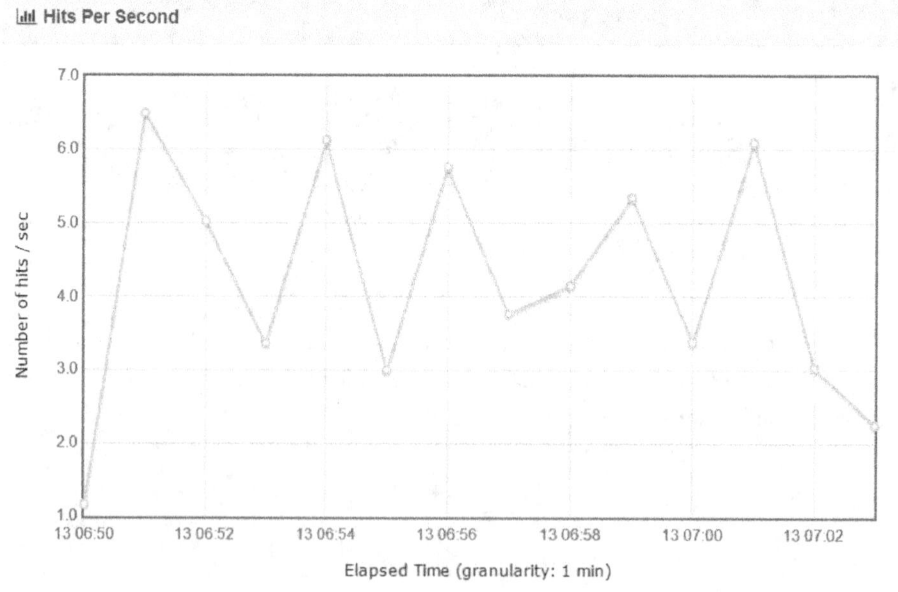

Figure 16: Apache JMeter Dashboard - Hits per second.

Figure 17 represents a sample Response Time Overview chart as provided by Apache JMeter Dashboard. The first column represents requests that were responded in less than 500 ms. As per Apdex index these represent the satisfied users. The second one is for requests between 500 ms to 1500 ms representing users with a tolerating user experience and third column represents requests taking longer than 1500 ms and classified under Apdex as frustrating requests.

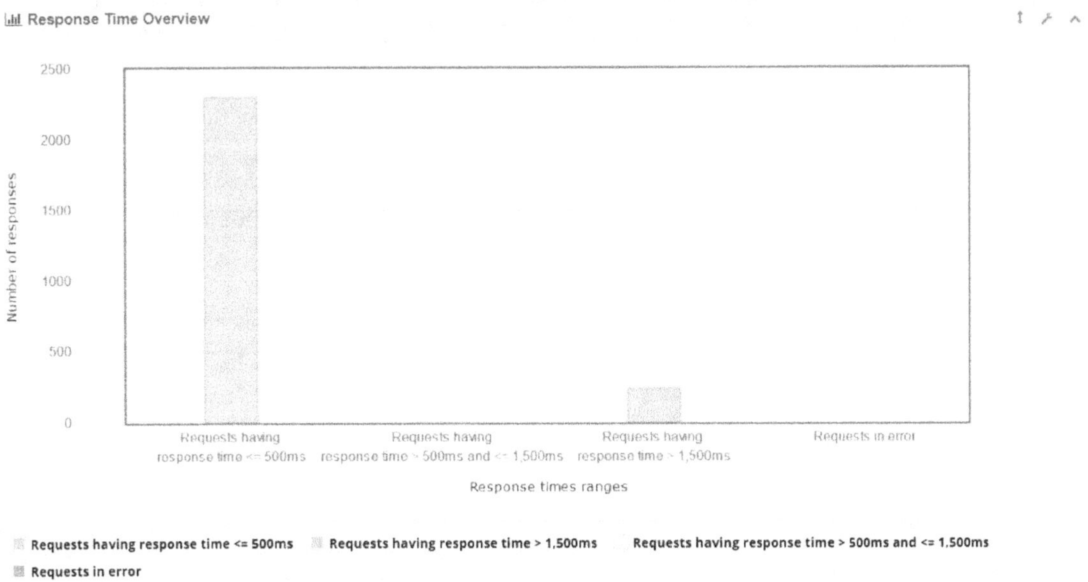

Figure 17: Apache JMeter Dashboard - Response Time Overview.

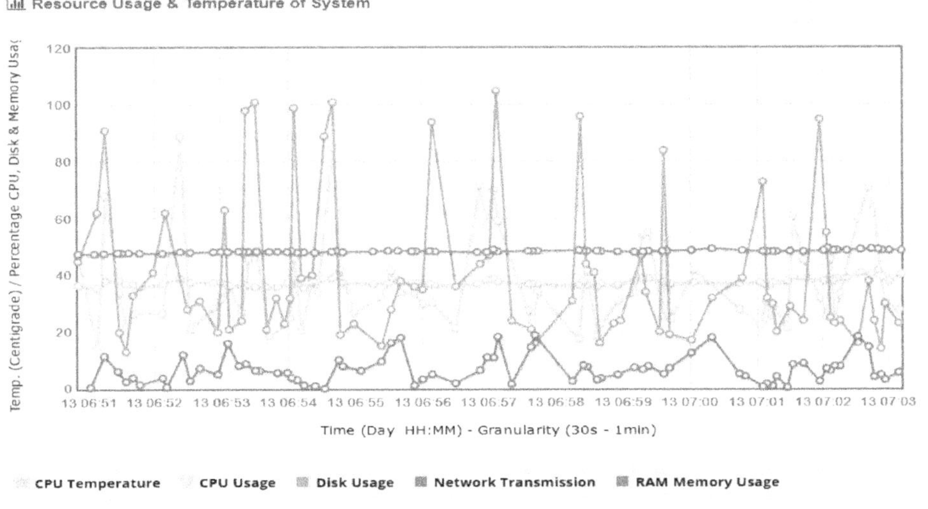

Figure 18: Apache JMETER - Resource usage.

Figure 18 shows a custom graph built for JMeter to measure the percentage usage of resources. The detailed apache reports are available on https://progressivewebserver.com/ under the spicy Moodlebox link (Dhuny, Spicy MoodleBox, 2021). The table on the mentioned website provides access to a detailed Apache JMeter Dashboard reports for consultation.

From Figure 18, it is observed that disk usage periodically gets high. In this chart the values are exceeding 100 because it uses 'iostats' to get disk activity. At times minor delays in computing provides results more or less than a second. This leads to a percentage higher than 100% which can be safely rounded to 100%. To solve this issue, it is recommended to run the Operating System on an SSD or a fast disk.

Resource usage monitoring is one way to identify which resource is mostly in demand. By default, Apache JMeter does not have such a graph. These can be added in JMeter through the use of plugins

5 UPGRADING TO SOLID STATE DISKS

RPI4 by default does not boot on an external disk or USB. It is well known though that faster disks can improve the performance of the system. James Chambers (Chambers, 2021) did provide an extensive documentation on his website on how to run the OS from an SSD. One of the major problems that lead to poor performance is USB Adapter chipset. It is a good idea to visit his website and cross check the known working adapters before purchasing one.

A summary on how to install an SSD is as follows:

- Connect your SSD to the computer you used to clone the original Moodlebox image and clone a copy of same disk image again on your disk.
- Connect the SSD to your RPI 4 which is already running. Open SSH / putty.
- Follow the steps on *https://jamesachambers.com/raspberry-pi-4-usb-boot-config-guide-for-ssd-flash-drives/* and check if a Quirk is required. If so, apply the same.
- Change the PARTUUID of the disk by using the **sudo fdisk /dev/sda.**
- Type **p** followed by **x** then **i.** Enter a new disk identifier. It should start with 0x followed by numeric values or letters a,c,b,d,e,f. The length should be 10 characters in total for example: 0xcccc1111.
- Press **x**, followed by **r** and **w** to finalize disk.
- This exercise simply changes the partition id of the disk to a unique value we may call.
- To check the PARTUUID, type **sudo blkid** on shell.
- Backup the cmdline.txt with **sudo cp /boot/cmdline.txt /boot/cmdline.txt.bkp.**
- Edit the current cmdline.txt by using **sudo nano /boot/cmdline.txt**
- Change the new PARTUUID to the new one created. For example: cccc1111-02.
- Do not forget to remove the 0x and add the -02 at the end to indicate use second partition.
- If the usb-storage quirk is required, do not forget to add same at the beginning of the line.
- To check which disk is being used, the following commands helps: **findmnt -n -o SOURCE /.**
- Currently, it should return **/dev/mmcblk0p2**, indicating that the OS is on SD Card

- **Reboot** by **typing sudo init 6** and check the mount point again it should display **/dev/sda2.**

*Note: If upon reboot the device does not restart properly, switch off the RPI, remove the card and open the contents from another computer. Find the **cmdline.txt**, delete it and rename the **cmdline.txt.bkp** to **cmdline.txt**.*

- To finalize the boot from SSD, the file system table should be modified.
- In putty, type **sudo nano /etc/fstab.**
- **Change the value** of the **PARTUUID** ending with **-02**, set the value the one recently created.
- **Save** and **exit** with **CTRL + o** and **CTRL + x.**
- **Reboot** by **typing sudo init 6.**

Once the system boots properly, it is now using the SSD. The only problem is that the system is not using the SSD full disk capacity. This can be corrected through the use of fdisk.

- **On ssh / putty, type sudo fdisk /dev/sda.**
- Press on P, to print the partition details.
- Note the start value for /dev/sda1, for example it might start with 532…
- From the fdisk command line press **d, 2, n, p, 2** followed by the start number previously noted, 532…
- For last sector, **press enter** to accept the default and Press **N** and **w** to exit.
- Reboot by **typing sudo init 6.**
- Run the command **sudo resize2fs /dev/sda2.**
- To check the size of the disk with **df -h** for disk free in human readable format.

Note: When working with fdisk command, if you are not sure of your previous operations, press q to quit and restart the process again. Once w is pressed, fdisk will write to disk.

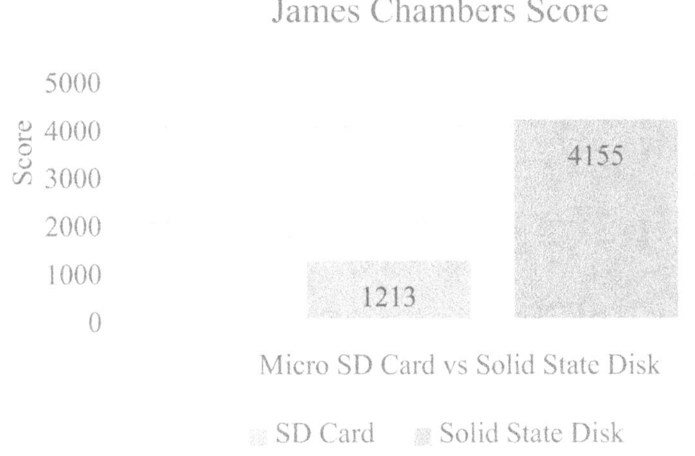

Figure 19: James Chambers score for SD Card vs Solid State Disk.

On the James Chambers score, when the SD card was compared against the SSD (Figure 19), it was observed that the SSD was more than 3x times faster than the SD card.

Perform the Moodle Benchmark test again and compare the overall score. For our tests, we did not find a major difference in score. Some operations of Moodle worked better with the SSD, like for example the *'Write course performance'* or the *'login times'* as shown in Figure 20.

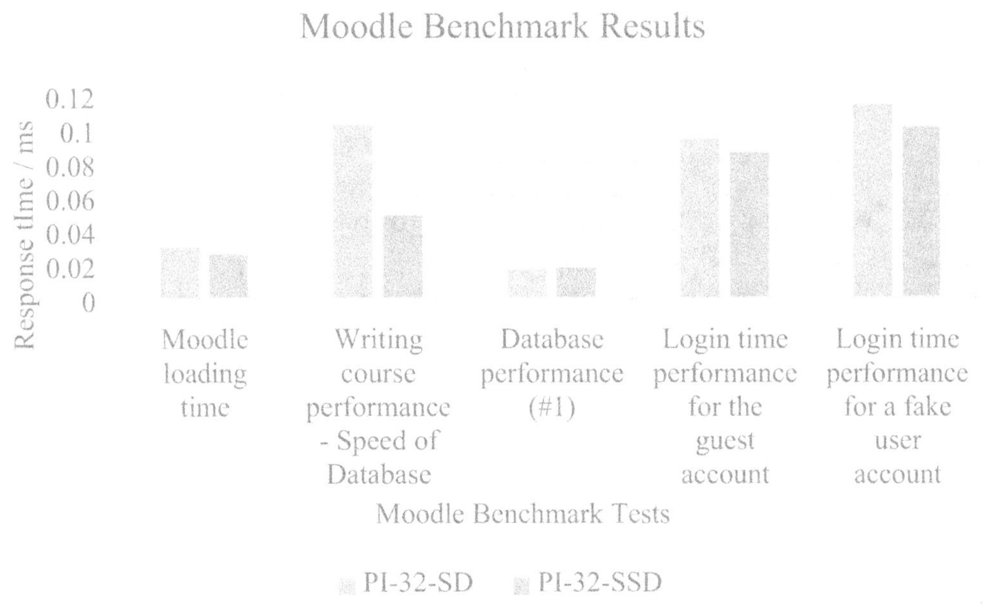

Figure 20: Moodle Benchmark tests.

6 UPGRADING TO 64-BIT OPERATING SYSTEM

On page 8, when the plugins were upgraded it was noted that Moodlebox was using a 32-bit version of Pi OS. There are many reports indicating that there are some performance gains when upgrading to 64-bit. It is also known that some systems may marginally benefit from an upgrade to a 64-bit OS. Here are some references for articles that one may find interesting to read (Raspberrypi.org, 2019), (Croce, 2020), (Williams, 2020) and (Longbottom, 2020).

There are two ways to move to a 64-bit OS
- Change the kernel parameters of Pi OS 32-bit to 64-bit.
- Install a 64-bit OS and install all the applications.

Change the kernel parameters to boot to Pi OS 64-bit
Open SSH or putty and type the following command to get the current OS,
- Type **uname -m**
- If the result starts with armv7, this indicates a 32-bit OS.
- Edit the config.txt file with **sudo /boot/config.txt**
- Add the following under the **[pi4]** section: **arm_64bit=1**
- Save and exit with CTRL + o and CTRL + x
- **Reboot** by typing **sudo init 6**.
- Type **uname -m** again to check the OS
- The output should now be aarch64 indicating 64-bit OS kernel running.

Perform the Moodle Benchmark test again on the 64-bit OS and compare the results. With Moodlebox version 3.10.0 update 2021-03-25 it was noted that the CPU processing speed was 0.962 and the score was 183 points. It is observed that the 64-bit OS did not improve the Pi OS environment for Moodle. In fact, on a 64-bit OS, the applications running should do so with their 64-bit binaries and not the 32-bit versions in order to have performance gains.

Installing a 64-bit OS and all its applications
The second approach that remains is download install and use a native 64-bit operating system. Ubuntu offers the 64-bit for arm architecture including a Long-Term Support (LTS) version with support for many years. The current version at the time of writing is 20.04.2 and is available on Ubuntu website (Ubuntu, 2021).

To install Ubuntu Server 20.04 LTS, you may need a micro HDMI cable, mouse and keyboard to connect to your Raspberry Pi.

- Download the 64-bit version from Ubuntu website.
- Use Balena Etcher to burn same to the SD Card.
- Connect the SD card to your RPI and boot the same.
- Once booted, type **sudo apt update && sudo apt upgrade -y** to update the system
- Install git using **sudo apt install git**.

Installing and configuring Moodle with all their services might take a long time to perform in order to produce a work similar to Moodlebox. Another approach is to make use of ansible which is an automation tool to run scripts on shell in order to perform appropriate tasks. Moodlebox's author, Nicolas Martignoni created some ansible scripts (Martignoni, Moodlebox Github, 2021) for Moodlebox that can be used instead of a custom install from scratch. The original script was ported for Ubuntu 64-bit and is available on (Dhuny, Spicy MoodleBox on Github, 2021).

To install the applications, follow the instruction below.

- On SSH / putty, type **git clone https://github.com/dhuny/spicyMoodlebox.git.**
- A folder spicyMoodlebox will appear in your work.
- Visit the READMe.md from the github repository and follow the instruction to install all the applications on the Ubuntu 64-bit.

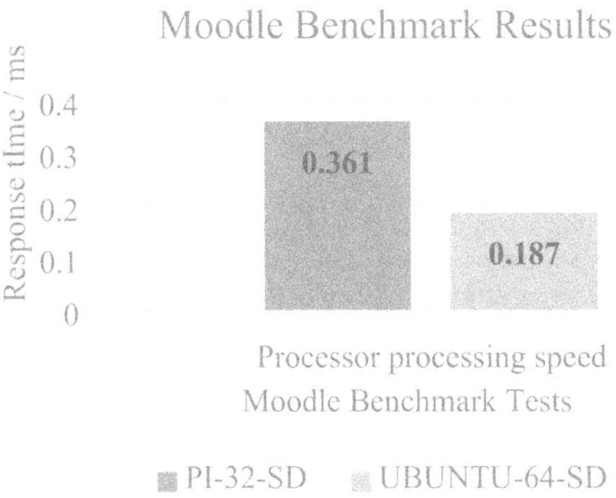

Figure 21: Moodle Benchmark results for Pi OS 32-bit vs Ubuntu 64-bit OS.

It is important to mention that in our test, the Processor processing speed of 64-bit OS improved tremendously but other sections of the Moodle Benchmark test were worse than the 64-bit OS.

7 HOME HOSTED LMS

Having a portable LMS is extremely handy for an educator. Same can be used in class to allow students to connect to the device for their lessons. The portability of Moodle is also useful for remote areas but there are situations where one would prefer to have its Moodle running at home to allow students to connect to the same via their internet connection at home. This method is most useful for countries with high internet penetration rate.

A good scenario is online teaching and learning during the pandemic. Many countries had educational institution closed down and educators were requested to perform online teaching. Moodle can easily support 30 simultaneous users at a time and can support up to 100 users but the user experience will be poor with too many simultaneous users.

With a small cohort size and a good internet connectivity it is easy to make Moodle accessible to the internet. Tests were carried out on a 20Mbps download and an 8Mbps upload speed Line with approximately 30 concurrent users and the system worked perfectly and is still on and working for more than one and a half years.

Home hosting solutions removes the hosting cost which would usually cost at least USD 100 per year. Apart from the cost, some providers do not allow the installation of external plugins. So, for example, it would be impossible to use the Interactive Content – H5P we reviewed in the previous chapter on some shared hosting. Another advantage is that the assignments are saved directly on a small computer sitting in the educators' premises. Review and marking exercises do not take long to download.

This section is dependent on hardware in use. The configurations will slightly vary according to the Internet Service Providers (ISP) and routers provided. The steps are provided here as a general guide. They involve 3 actions
1. Configure a Static IP Address for the Ethernet.
2. Open the IP Address to the external world through port forwarding.
3. Purchase a domain and perform a dynamic mapping.

Note: Before trying this section, make sure to change the username and password of your system

Configure a Static IP address

In this example, we will use a 32-bit Pi OS to configure a static IP

- Find and note the current IP address by using the **ifconfig** command.
- Edit the **/etc/dhcpcd.conf** using the command **sudo nano /etc/dhcpcd.conf**
- Remove the # comment and set the static ip_address, static routers and static domain_name_servers to appropriate values matching your network.
- Note the static IP address at it will be used on port forwarding in upcoming section.
- Restart the server.
- Check the IP address again with ifconfig.

Port Forwarding to your Web Server

Port forwarding steps are router specific. You will have to search on the internet how to do port forwarding on your box. By default, to connect to your router, you will type either 192.168.1.1, 192.168.1.0 or 192.168.100.1 depending on your router make. This information is provided in the user manual. The root IP will lead you to the login page to get access to the Admin control panel.

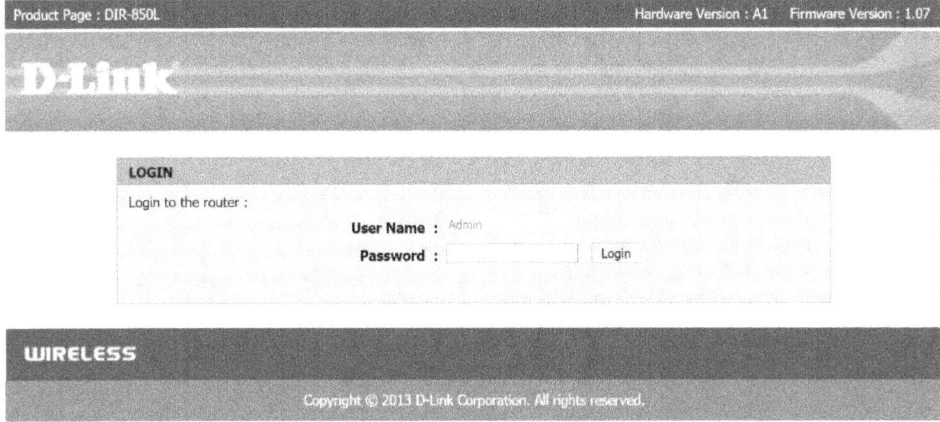

Figure 22: Admin panel for D-Link Routers.

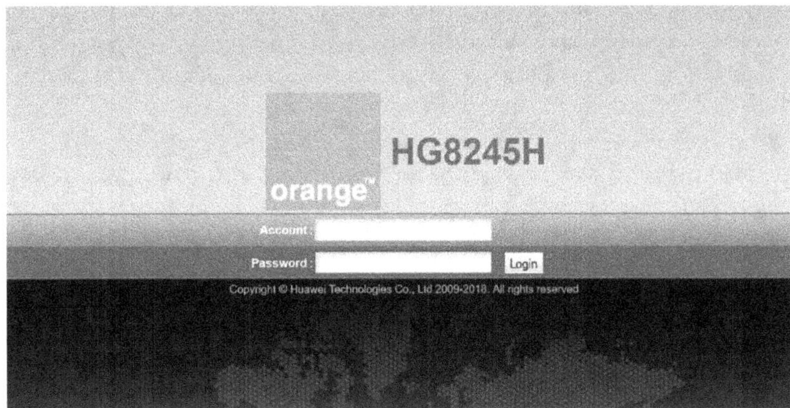

Figure 23: Admin panel for Huawei Routers.

Figure 22 and Figure 23 shows the admin panel interfaces for D-Link and the Huawei Routers. You may contact your service provider to recover lost passwords. From the Router Admin interface, you will have to configure the ports 80 and 443 to redirect to the static IP address set in previous section. Check your router's manual for same. Once done, save and restart the router.

To test if the changes are working properly, you will need to find your public IP address. Internet Speed tests tools like speedtest.net or speed.io shall provide the info. You won't be able to connect to your own device if you use the internet connectivity from your router. To test, use a mobile device with mobile data and switch off any Wi-Fi access point. A successful connection is identified by the ability of the server to connect to Moodle before the page design breaks because Moodle is configured to load the default domain name which is Moodlebox.home for Moodlebox.

One problem with the current IP address is that it changes periodically or when the router restarts. Another issue is that is would be inappropriate to share IP addresses as unique identifiers with users. Dynamic Domain Name Systems (DDNS) solves these problems.

Dynamic Domain Name Systems (DDNS)
There are so many DDNS providers available, the best way to identify which ones to work with is to check inside your Router. For example, the Huawei HG8245 has the DDNS settings for many providers. A search on YouTube for '*Setup DDNS on a Huawei Router (HG8245H)*' provides an example of the DDNS providers as well as their configuration. The original list of providers is:

- dyndns
- qdns
- gnudip
- no-ip
- dtdns
- easydns
- ORAY.

To configure the DDNS simply visit any of the providers, create an account and use the credentials to configure the DDNS section in the router Admin panel. Once the router IP address changes, the router will inform the DDNS that the existing IP present in its list should be updated.

DDNS allow users to create free subdomains with any name for mapping and offer paid service for a domain registration and mapping. You may want to test your Moodle with a free subdomain first. If everything goes fine then you can opt to purchase a domain.

It is important to mention that apart from the list present in the router DDNS section, there are many other providers. One good example is:

- dynu.com

The dynu.com website has configuration settings for the Huawei HG8245, 8346M and 8045H routers (dynu.com, 2021). The settings will use **dyndns-custom** as the Service Provider but the hostname will be the api of the dynu.com service. Dynu.com was tested and found to work properly.

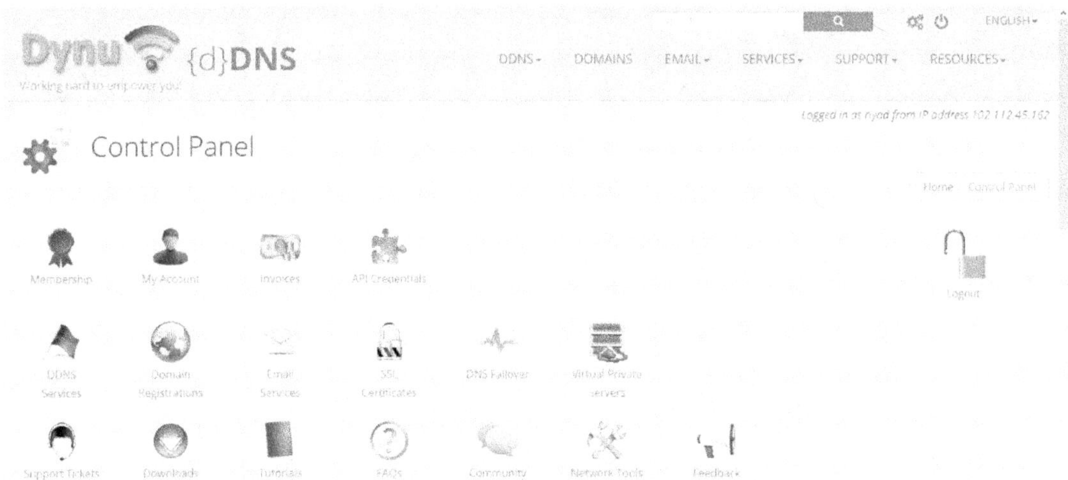

Figure 24: Admin panel of Dynu.com DDNS service provider.

Figure 24 shows that admin panel of Dynu.com as an example of services that are offered by DDNS providers. These include Domain registrations where domains can be purchased, DDNS services, Email services where domain specific email addresses can be forwarded to specific inboxes amongst others.

8 CONCLUSIONS

A Learning Management System (LMS) is a great tool for classroom management and is a useful repository for educational materials. The internet is already full of resources that educators can use to enhance learning. With the Interactive Content - H5P plugin, educators can simply pull a YouTube video link onto their Moodle LMS, add questions on top of the video and monitor the class progress. This changes the role of an educator to a facilitator. LMS make visible all individual progresses made by students and reduce the workload of educators. The pandemic accelerated teaching and learning and different tools were used. Unfortunately, not all LMSs are made equal, some have more tools and functionalities than others and Moodle excel in its field. Some educators never had the opportunity to see an LMS in action. Among the various reasons include cost and lack of necessary infrastructure. Raspberry Pi opens new doors for many areas including the use of LMS in the education sector.

The work of Nicolas Martignoni made it even easier to use Moodle with the preinstalled image ready to be deployed. The purpose of this book further builds on what is already available to make Moodle more accessible to educators.

This book helps explore a portable Moodle on a Raspberry Pi through Moodlebox. Then, readers discover the power of the plugin's world through the Interactive Content-H5P plugin. A taste of performance is provided with Moodle Benchmark, James Chambers and Apache JMeter. The portable LMS was upgraded to use SSD for those who want a better average response time from the Box. For users who want to explore the custom installation of their own Moodle on a Ubuntu 64-bit OS, an ansible script was available. Finally, for those who doesn't want Moodle to be portable but instead needs Moodle at home behind their router and accessible via the internet, there is the Home Hosted LMS chapter to explains make to make this possible.

To conclude, a Moodle on a Raspberry Pi is worth a try.

9 REFERENCES

(2018). Retrieved from Sourceforge.net: https://sourceforge.net/projects/win32diskimager/

Apache JMeter. (2021). Retrieved from Apache JMeter: https://jmeter.apache.org/download_jmeter.cgi

balena. (2021). *Balena Etcher*. Retrieved from balena.io: https://www.balena.io/etcher/

Chambers, J. (2021). *Raspberry Pi 4 USB Boot Config Guide for SSD / Flash Drives*. Retrieved from jameschambers.com: https://jamesachambers.com/raspberry-pi-4-usb-boot-config-guide-for-ssd-flash-drives/

Croce, M. (2020). *Why you should run a 64 bit OS on your Raspberry Pi4*. Retrieved March 19, 2021, from https://matteocroce.medium.com/why-you-should-run-a-64-bit-os-on-your-raspberry-pi4-bd5290d48947

de Castro, J. (2021). *Treasure Hunt*. Retrieved from jucas.github.io: https://juacas.github.io/moodle-mod_treasurehunt/install.html

de Castro, J., Rodríguez, A., Verdú, M., Regueras, L., Merino, F., Molina, I., . . . Ramos, J. (2021). Georeferenced Learning Activities: An Experience with Moodle. *EdMedia + Innovate Learning* (pp. 160-168). Amsterdam: Association for the Advancement of Computing in Education (AACE). Retrieved from https://juacas.github.io/moodle-mod_treasurehunt/

Dhuny, R. (2021). *Spicy MoodleBox*. Retrieved from Progressive Web Server: https://progressivewebserver.com/?page_id=37#apdex

Dhuny, R. (2021). *Spicy MoodleBox on Github*. Retrieved February 26, 2021, from Github Repository: https://github.com/dhuny/spicyMoodlebox

dynu.com. (2021). *HUAWEI HG8245/8346M/8045H*. Retrieved from dynu.com: https://www.dynu.com/DynamicDNS/IPUpdateClient/HUAWEI-HG8245-HG8346M-

HG8045H

Kraemer, K. L., Dedrick, J., & Sharma, P. (2011). One Laptop Per Child (OLPC): A Novel Computerization Movement? *44th Hawaii International Conference on System Sciences* (pp. 1-10). Kauai, HI, USA: IEEE.

Longbottom, R. (2020). *Raspberry Pi 64 Bit OS and 8 GB Pi 4B Benchmarks.* Retrieved from https://www.researchgate.net/publication/342232830_Raspberry_Pi_64_Bit_OS_and_8_GB_Pi_4B_Benchmarks

Martignoni, N. (2021). *Moodlebox Github.* Retrieved from Github: https://github.com/moodlebox/moodlebox

Martignoni, N., & Pannequin, M. (2020). *Reports: Moodle Benchmark.* Retrieved October 28, 2020, from Moodle: https://moodle.org/plugins/report_benchmark

Moodlebox. (2020). *Campus "MoodleBox in detention" winner.* Retrieved October 20, 2020, from https://moodlebox.net/en/news/moodlebox-in-detention/

Moodlebox. (2021). *Moodlebox.* Retrieved from Moodlebox: https://moodlebox.net/

Petterson, F., Marstrander, T., Jørgensen, P., With, G., & Svein-Tore. (2021). *Activities: Interactive Content – H5P.* Retrieved from moodle.org/plugins/mod_hvp: https://moodle.org/plugins/mod_hvp

pimoroni. (2021). *Raspberry Pi4 Model B.* Retrieved from Pimoroni online shop: https://shop.pimoroni.com/products/raspberry-pi-4?variant=29157087445075

Raghav Pal. (2016). *JMeter Beginner Tutorial 1 - How to install Jmeter.* Retrieved from https://automationstepbystep.com/: https://www.youtube.com/watch?v=M-iAXz8vs48&t=61s

Raspberry Pi. (2021). *Install Raspberry Pi OS using Raspberry Pi Imager.* Retrieved from raspberrypi.org: https://www.raspberrypi.org/software/

Raspberrypi.org. (2019). *Tutorial: How (and why!) to set up a 64-bit kernel, 32-bit Raspbian host OS, 64-bit nspawn Debian guest OS RPi3 system.* Retrieved October 07, 2020, from Raspberry Pi: https://www.raspberrypi.org/forums/viewtopic.php?t=232415

raspberrypi.org. (2021). *Raspberry Pi 4.* Retrieved from raspberrypi.org: https://www.raspberrypi.org/products/raspberry-pi-4-model-b/

Tatham, S., Lanes, A., Harris, B., & Nevins, J. (2020). *Download PuTTY: latest release (0.74)*. Retrieved from www.chiark.greenend.org.uk: https://www.chiark.greenend.org.uk/~sgtatham/putty/latest.html

Ubuntu. (2021). *Install Ubuntu on a Raspberry Pi*. Retrieved from ubuntu.com: https://ubuntu.com/download/raspberry-pi

Williams, A. (2020). *How to Make Your Raspberry Pi 4 Faster with a 64 Bit Kernel*. Retrieved from medium.com: https://medium.com/for-linux-users/how-to-make-your-raspberry-pi-4-faster-with-a-64-bit-kernel-77028c47d653

ABOUT THE AUTHOR

Dhuny Riyad is an academic member of the School of Innovative Technologies and Engineering (SITE) at the University of Technology, Mauritius (UTM) and is currently the Head of Department of Creative Arts, Film and Media Technologies (CAFMT). Riyad explored many Learning Management Systems (LMS) and even wrote his own software before finally adopting Moodle some 10 years back. Riyad is optimist on the impact of a portable LMS can have on education, especially in remote areas and would like to help accelerate its adoption. His main field is Software Engineering with a strong affinity for Linux and Web Development in general.

Feel free to get in touch with the author for projects in his field of interest.